Riches of the Earth

Salt

Irene Franck and David Brownstone

GROLIER

An imprint of Scholastic Library Publishing
Danbury, Connecticut

Credits and Acknowledgments

abbreviations: t (top), b (bottom), l (left), r (right), c (center)

Image credits: Agricultural Research Service Library: 14l (Scott Bauer), 17; Getty Images: 1 (Nino Mascardi/Image Bank), 4 (Rita Maas/Image Bank), 28 (Mark Joseph/Stone); Getty Images/PhotoDisc: 5 (Duncan Smith); 12, 13, and 29 (PhotoLink); 16 (Ryan McVay), 18 (John A. Rizzo); National Aeronautics and Space Administration (NASA): 1t and running heads; National Geographic Society: 3 (James L. Amos), 6l (Bruce Dale), 6r (John E. Fletcher), 24t and 25 (Volkmar Wentzel); Photo Researchers, Inc.: 7 (Science Photo Library/R. E. Litchfield), 8 (Science Photo Library/Peter Falkner), 9 (Charles D. Winters), 10 (David R. Frazier Photolibrary), 11 (Noah Poritz), 14r (Tim Davis), 15 (Will and Deni McIntyre); 22, 23, 24b, and 27 (Georg Gerster); The Salt Institute: 26; Woodfin Camp & Associates: 20 (Loren McIntyre); World Bank: 19 (Curt Carnemark). Original images drawn for this book by K & P Publishing Services: 21.

Our thanks to Joe Hollander, Phil Friedman, and Laurie McCurley at Scholastic Library Publishing; to photo researchers Susan Hormuth, Robin Sand, and Robert Melcak; to copy editor Michael Burke; and to the librarians throughout the northeastern library network, in particular to the staff of the Chappaqua Library—director Mark Hasskarl; the expert reference staff, including Martha Alcott, Michele J. Capozzella, Maryanne Eaton, Catherine Paulsen, Jane Peyraud, Paula Peyraud, and Carolyn Reznick; and the circulation staff, headed by Barbara Le Sauvage—for fulfilling our wide-ranging research needs.

Published 2003 by Grolier
Division of Scholastic Library Publishing
Old Sherman Turnpike
Danbury, Connecticut 06816

For information address the publisher:
Scholastic Library Publishing, Grolier Division
Old Sherman Turnpike, Danbury, Connecticut 06816

© 2003 Irene M. Franck and David M. Brownstone

Library of Congress Cataloging-in-Publication Data

Franck, Irene M.
   Salt / Irene Franck and David Brownstone.
     p. cm. -- (Riches of the earth ; v. 10)
   Summary: Provides information about salt and its importance in everyday life.
   Includes bibliographical references and index.
   ISBN 0-7172-5730-4 (set : alk. paper) -- ISBN 0-7172-5722-3 (vol. 10 : alk paper)
     1. Salt--Juvenile literature [1. Salt.] I. Brownstone, David M. II. Title.

TN900.F73 2003
622'.3632--dc21

2003044086

Printed in the United States of America

Designed by K & P Publishing Services

Contents

White Gold

Today a shaker of salt is commonplace on almost every dining table, and we take salt for granted. But in many times and places in the past, salt could be the key to riches and power. It was so precious that it was sometimes called "white gold."

For people throughout history salt has meant the difference between sickness and health, between being rich and poor, sometimes even between peace and war.

Salt is so important to us that we can die if our bodies have too much or too little of it. Salt certainly makes many foods taste better, but more important, we must have some salt daily to replace what we lose. Otherwise our bodies will not function properly (see p. 12).

Some countries have been rich because they had salt. That is because people without salt are so eager to get some that they will pay almost anything for it. At some times and places in history, salt has literally been worth its weight—or more—in gold (see p. 19). That's why salt has sometimes been called "white gold."

Salt has also helped shape human history. All over the world people have fought to gain control of salt deposits and saltworks. One of Rome's earliest conquests (probably in the 600s B.C.) was the coastal saltworks at Ostia, at the mouth of Italy's Tiber River. The Romans then went on to build a vast empire with many famous roads, but the one between Ostia and Rome was the first major road they built, called the Via Salaria—the Salt Way.

Salt was also essential to the major explorations that took Europeans around the world. Humans had long used salt to preserve foods (see p. 17). Earlier explorers had generally hugged the coastline, so they could catch, gather, or buy fresh foods along the way. However, explorers such as Columbus set off across vast oceans, not knowing when they and their crews would again see land. They carried with them enough provisions, primarily salted meat, to last them a year or more.

Salt is made of sodium and chlorine (see p. 6). With the development of modern industry, both sodium and chlorine became a key part of many manufacturing processes—which often start with simple salt.

Traditionally salt was often kept in a small dish (called a *saltcellar*), rather than in a shaker. Cooks in the kitchen or diners at the table would take pinches or spoonfuls of the salt as needed in cooking or eating.

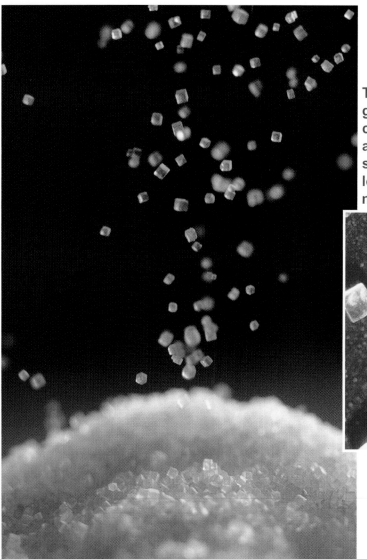

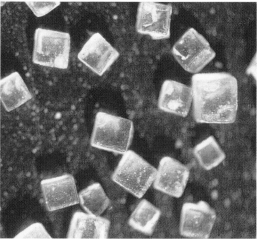

The high-speed electronic photograph at the left shows a stream of common table salt, cascading into a pile. You can see the individual salt crystals as tiny cubes, both at left and in the even more highly magnified view below.

What Is Salt?

Pure sodium is a silvery-white metal, so soft that you can cut it with a knife—but if it comes into contact with water, it will burst into flame! Pure chlorine is a yellowish-green poisonous gas, used as a military weapon in World War I. However, if you put sodium and

chlorine together as sodium chloride, the result is common table salt.

In fact, you would not find pure sodium or pure chlorine outside a laboratory or factory. Both join so readily with other substances that they form many different kinds of compounds (mixed substances).

The best-known of these compounds is table salt: sodium chloride. (In chemistry many other kinds of compounds are known as salts, but in everyday life when people say simply "salt," they mean sodium chloride.)

Salt is a crystal, which is a solid form with flat, regularly repeating sides. For salt the crystal form is a cube, a boxlike shape with equal square sides all around. Pure salt crystals are clear and colorless. However, the salt crystals we use are generally white (though some can be brownish or grayish) because they contain some impurities or deliberately added materials (see p. 26).

If the salt crystal forms on a surface of water, it can take a different form. Then it grows in a treelike branching crystal (called a *hopper crystal*), looking much like frost forming on a window. These much softer crystals are called *flake salt*.

Salt in Water

Salt dissolves readily in water—and that is the main place where it is found. Saltwater seas cover more

This is a different kind of salt crystal, growing in a treelike form, like frost on a window. These crystals are much softer than regular salt crystals, so the product is called *flake salt*.

In hot places with little rainfall, bodies of water often evaporate away, leaving behind salt deposits. You can see the old shoreline of Lake Carson in western Nevada.

than 70 percent of the Earth's surface, and salt makes up about 3 percent of this seawater. The percentage of salt is lower near the North and South Poles and higher in partly enclosed seas like the Mediterranean and Red Seas. It is even higher in some inland salt lakes, such as the Dead Sea between Israel and Jordan. Our modern salt supply comes from today's saltwater seas or from ancient ones that have long since dried up.

Over many millions of years the Earth's surface has changed greatly. Though we are not usually aware of it, large plates (sections) of the Earth's crust—the outer part of Earth that we live on—are moving in extremely slow motion (except during earthquakes!). Some plates are lifted up, while others sink. The water level of the oceans also changes as the Earth's climate gets warmer or colder. The result is that the land includes many areas that formerly were the floors of saltwater seas. As the seas dried out, water evaporated (went into the air), leaving behind salt.

You cannot see salt dissolved in saltwater. However, as the water evaporates, the amount of salt increases. When the water becomes salty enough, the salt begins to form crystals. Chemists call this process *precipitation*. Eventually, unless more fresh water is added, the body of water dries up completely. Then only the salt remains, along with any other substances that had been dissolved in the water.

Many such dried-up seabeds can be seen on the surface of the Earth, often called *salt flats*. Bonneville Salt Flats, part of Utah's Great Salt Lake Desert, is so flat that it is used for setting speed records. The nearby Great Salt Lake, once part of a much larger saltwater sea, is itself shrinking and slowly drying up.

In the very long period of geological time, some such ancient seabeds on land were covered over by soil and other materials. The result is that vast stores of salt are buried deep underground in the form of rock salt, which chemists call *halite*.

When a solution contains enough salt, crystals of sodium chloride will begin to form, a process called *precipitation*. That is just what is happening in this test tube.

Salt flats are some of the flattest, driest places in the world, sometimes used for automobile races and speed trials. These are salt flats at Death Valley in California.

As the Earth's crustal plates move around, some underground salt deposits have been forced up between other rocks to or near the surface. These are called *salt domes*. Humans have mined some such salt domes for thousands of years (see p. 24). Many other salt domes have been discovered in modern times, especially by petroleum geologists, because underground pools of highly valuable petroleum (oil) are often found nearby.

Some salt deposits come into contact with water being forced upward from underground lakes or streams. As the water rises, it dissolves and takes with it some salt from the rocks. The brine (salt solution) reaches the surface as *salt springs* or *brine springs*. These, too, have long been key sources of salt.

Rainwater and surface water also dissolve salt from surface rocks. Some of this flows into ponds or lakes that dry up seasonally, providing more sources of surface salt. The rest of the briny water flows downhill, eventually adding more salt to the sea.

If a body of water contains enough salt, solid crystals of salt will begin to form. These are mounds of salt precipitating out of water in a salt evaporation pond on Mexico's Baja Peninsula.

What's in a Name?

Salt is an old name for a common substance. The word *salt* goes back at least to Roman times. The road to Rome's early saltworks was called the Via Salaria (see p. 5), and the Romans' god of health was named Salus. Roman soldiers received some of their pay as salt; that part was called the *salarium*, from which we get the modern word *salary*. Many European sites of saltworks have some variant of the word in their name, such as Salzburg in Austria. Another related word is *salami*, one of the many foods preserved and flavored with salt (see p. 17).

The ancient Greeks knew both salt and the saltwater sea by the name *hals*. From this we get our name for rock salt: *halite*. The word root *hal-* is also found in the names of many early saltworks. Among them is Austria's Hallstatt, a key archaeological site where a prehistoric salt mine has been found (see p. 24).

Only in recent centuries did scientists learn that salt was made up of the elements (basic substances) sodium and chlorine. Sodium was first isolated by British chemist Humphry Davy in 1807. Its chemical abbreviation is *Na*, for *natron*, a French word for a kind of salt. Chlorine was first manufactured in the laboratory by Swedish chemist Carl Wilhelm Scheele in 1774. It was abbreviated *Cl*, so the chemical abbreviation for salt is *NaCl*.

People who do hard work or heavy exercise out in the sun, like this mountain biker, have to be careful that they do not sweat too much and become dehydrated.

Salt for Life

Some people have described the body as an ocean surrounded by skin. That is not as strange as it might sound. About 70 percent of the body's weight is fluid—and salty fluid at that.

Inside the body salt is dissolved in these fluids. When that happens, sodium and chlorine separate to perform different jobs.

Chlorine is found in many body fluids. However, its main job is in the stomach. There it joins with hydrogen to form hydrochloric acid. This helps us to digest food—that is, to break food down so the body can use it.

Sodium has more central and wide-ranging jobs. It is found in most of the body's fluids, including blood, sweat, tears, mothers' breast milk, and the fluids that constantly

Many of our most popular and favorite foods are loaded with salt. That includes the hot dog, mustard, pickles, olives, and potato chips pictured here.

bathe the cells that make up our bodies and keep us alive. One of sodium's most important functions is to help fluids move into and out of those cells.

The body has an elaborate system of checks and balances to maintain the levels of sodium in these fluids. The kidneys are the main organ controlling this. If the body has too much sodium, special chemicals called *hormones* remove some sodium and send it out of the body in urine. They also tell the body to get more water, a signal we feel as thirst. If the body has too little salt, hormones signal the kidneys to hold on to sodium and get rid of some water.

The body loses small amounts of sodium every day, especially through sweat. The amount varies with the person. Someone doing hard labor or heavy exercise on a hot day will lose a lot of sodium. Someone resting in the cool shade will lose less.

Whatever the amount, the body requires some salt daily to replace what is lost. Peoples whose diets are heavy in meats get all the sodium they need from their food. Arctic peoples who eat mostly meat, for example, do not generally feel the need to add salt to their food.

However, for many thousands of years most humans have had a more varied diet, including large amounts of grains and vegetables. More healthy in many ways, this diet does not provide all the salt our bodies need. The result is that most people feel a hunger for salt. The taste buds in our mouths recognize only a handful of tastes, but one of them is saltiness. This helps our bodies to identify when a food is salty and likely to provide needed sodium.

Humans are not alone in needing sodium. Animals that live mainly on plants (*herbivores*) also feel sodium hunger. They will travel great distances to get the salt they need. Some of the oldest pathways in the

Humans are not alone in their need for salt. Many other animals, especially those that eat mostly plants, are drawn to salt licks, places where the water or ground contains the salt that they need. This elephant is digging for salt in Kenya's Aberdare National Park.

Beings of all shapes and sizes are attracted by salt. This sweat bee, shown on a flower, is so named because it is attracted to salty sweat, as on your skin on a hot day.

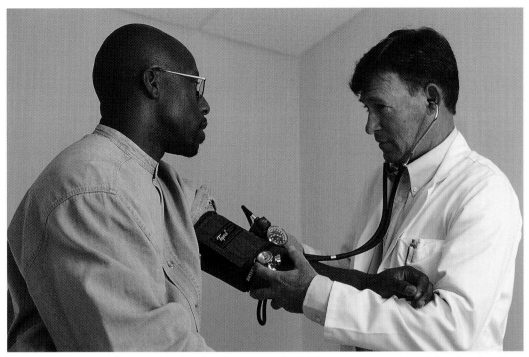

Having too much salt in the body can raise blood pressure. This doctor is using a medical device to take his patient's blood pressure.

Americas, for example, were made not by humans but by animals such as deer and buffalo going to and from sources of salt (and water).

Areas with surface salt deposits are called *salt licks* because the animals literally lick the rocks for the salt, sometimes digging at the soil to get it. Humans, too, have often settled near sources of salt, useful for both themselves and their livestock. People now sometimes put out blocks of salt for livestock and other animals.

Too Much, Too Little

Today most humans get far more salt than they need. Many of our favorite foods are loaded with salt. This makes most foods more tasty. The problem is that the body's kidneys sometimes cannot handle the excess of salt. When that happens, salt builds up in the body's fluids, and the body holds on to extra water to try to balance that excess salt. That causes the blood to move through the body's blood delivery system (the *cardiovascular system*) with more force. That, in turn, puts more pressure on the arteries, veins, heart, and kidneys that carry, pump, and filter the blood, and in the long run can damage them. This condition is called *hypertension* or *high blood pressure.*

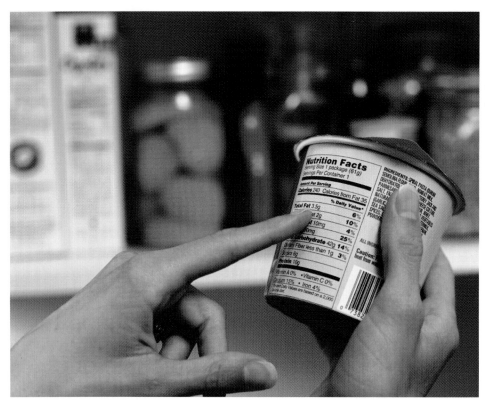

To find out how much salt is in a product, you can check the nutritional label on the back of it, as on this container.

In extreme cases, as the body tries to hold on to water to lessen the fluids' saltiness, the body stops sweating. This shuts down its cooling system. Meanwhile toxic (poisonous) substances that are normally flushed out in urine remain in the kidneys. These and other effects can cause death. That is why saltwater sailors must carry fresh water for drinking. Seawater is far too salty for the body to handle.

Too little sodium can also cause serious problems. People who exercise or work hard on a hot day can lose a lot of fluid through sweat. Sodium can also be lost during some illnesses, such as diarrhea, or in cases of severe shock. Loss of too much water from the body leads to a condition called *dehydration*.

Drinking water helps, but water alone cannot replace the salt and other key substances lost in sweat. Sometimes people take salt tablets. Today athletes and workers often drink specially formulated fluids to replace what has been lost. In severe cases of dehydration, saline (salt) solutions are given intravenously (fed by needle directly into a vein) to maintain the body's fluids. Otherwise the body's internal mechanisms can go awry, causing severe illness and even death.

Many foods are processed and preserved with salt. The lunch meats on this platter are "cured" with salt, which also plays a key role in turning cucumbers into pickles like the one shown here.

Preserving Food

Salt makes almost all foods taste better. However, for many centuries salt has also been used to preserve foods.

From the earliest times humans had to find ways to preserve foods beyond just a few days. Many foods spoil very quickly. Preserving methods had to stop the growth of bacteria and other organisms that can cause the food to spoil.

One very early way to do this was to dry foods in the air and sun or in the oven. However, the preferred way of preserving many foods was to salt them, a process called *curing*. Salt actually works partly by drying the food, since it draws water out, leaving none for the bacteria.

Some foods would be heavily rubbed with salt on the outside and then dried out and perhaps smoked, such as a ham. Some foods would be soaked and stored in a brine (salt solution), such as olives and pickles. Other foods would be ground up and mixed with salt, like the many kinds of sausages.

For long-term storage meats and fish were packed in salt. This tended to make them very hard, so they would have to be soaked and cooked a long time before eating. However, if salted properly, they could last for months.

In the age of exploration starting in the 1400s, one reason that ships were able to sail far from land was that they carried stores of salted meat and fish for food. In the centuries of expansion that followed, many overland pioneers also carried salted provisions.

Salting allowed fishing boats to go far from shore in search of new fishing grounds. They carried large stores of salt with them because, for proper preservation, the fish they caught had to be salted within 24 hours.

Until the development of modern refrigerators, salting remained a main way of preserving foods. And even today, when refrigerators are widespread, many salted foods remain widely popular, such as salami, smoked salmon (lox), pickles, and olives soaked in brine.

Smoked salmon (lox) is preserved by salting. Though we have refrigeration today, the salmon is still made the traditional way because it tastes so good, often with cream cheese on a bagel, as shown here.

Getting Salt

Working in salt mines has always been hard, exhausting, and often dirty work. Constant exposure to salt can cause sores to open up on the skin. This man is working in a salt mine in Irian Jaya, in the island nation of Indonesia.

Today salt is cheap and readily available to most people, but that has been true only in recent centuries. For many centuries salt was so valuable it was sometimes called "white gold." Sometimes salt was traded for gold, pound for pound, and sometimes it was worth twice as much as gold! Writing in the 500s A.D., Roman historian Cassiodorus put it this way: "Mankind can live without gold but not without salt."

Countries that had salt became rich because they could trade it for other things they wanted. Salt-poor countries had to trade other valuable items for the precious salt. Peoples and nations went to war over saltworks and salt deposits. For many centuries all over the world, governments taxed salt and tried to control salt production. The oldest known tax on salt dates back to 2200 B.C. in China.

Salt was even used as a form of money, as it still is unofficially in some regions, notably in parts of Africa. Sometimes it was even used as official money, traded in standard blocks with an imperial stamp

Where there is plenty of sun and little rainfall, salt can be evaporated right on the seacoast, as on the coastal salt flats of Colombia, where the Guajiro people get salt from seawater.

on it, as Marco Polo reported on his visit to China in the 1200s.

Sea Salt

People who live on seacoasts have always had ready access to salt. In regions with plenty of sunshine and not too much rainfall, people could get salt directly from the sea. They would pour seawater into small, shallow evaporation ponds and let the sun evaporate some of it. When the pond water became salty enough, salt crystals would begin to precipitate out (see p. 9). Then workers had only to rake out the salt, called *solar salt*, *sea salt*, or *bay salt*. This salt could be used locally or traded to others for desired goods.

Coastal people who had too little sunshine or too much rainfall could take a different approach. They boiled seawater in large vats until salt crystals began to form. Boiling was a rather inexpensive process where cheap fuel, such as wood or later coal, was available.

People who lived near brine springs (see p. 10) could also get salt by boiling. One of the most famous brine springs in Europe was

Notable sources of salt, past and present

at Lüneburg in northern Germany. Its salt was heavily used in preserving fish for the northern European fishing industry.

Another way to get salt, widely used in the Netherlands, was to burn *peat* (matted masses of partly decayed vegetable matter) from saltwater bogs. Chunks of peat were cut out and stored until dry enough and then burned. The ashes were mixed with seawater to dissolve out the salt, and the ashes were then filtered out. The resulting brine was then boiled to form salt crystals.

Sea salt was not all the same, because seawater is not all the same. Different kinds of substances (besides salt) are dissolved in the water, some desirable, some not. As scientific techniques developed in later centuries, people learned to recognize the substances dissolved in seawater. These precipitated out of the water at different points in the evaporation process. Those that precipitated out first could be removed quickly, so they did not contaminate the desired salt. And salt itself could be taken out as soon

In Ethiopia's Danakil Depression workers still use primitive sticks to pry up slabs of salt. These are then cut up into standard sizes (see center background) for transport and sale.

as it formed, before other unwanted substances began to precipitate out.

Solar salt was less desirable than sea salt obtained by boiling. That is because coastal seawater often contained bits of animal and plant matter and other undesirable trash, which remained after evaporation. Salt obtained by boiling was purer.

Surface Salt

Some people lived near surface salt deposits, the remains of ancient seas (see p. 7), often found in desert country. However, getting the salt out of these deposits was—and is— hard work, generally made more difficult by hot, dry conditions.

The surface salt mines at Taghaza, in the western region of Africa's Sahara Desert, were for many centuries worked by slaves. The region was so desolate that every bit of food and water for the slaves and the salt traders had to be carried in by camel caravan. However, the mining was profitable because many people in West Africa, just to the south, had no salt but plenty of gold.

In the famous "silent trade," the salt traders would place slabs of salt on a riverbank and then withdraw. The West Africans would put what they considered a fair amount of gold beside the salt. If the traders were satisfied, they took the gold and left the salt. Otherwise the two sides adjusted their "offers" until both were satisfied—without a word being said.

Later regular markets grew. One of the most famous was in Timbuktu, established in about 1000 A.D. on the edge of the Sahara Desert in what is now Mali. Caravans still bring to the region slabs of salt mined in the Sahara.

Across the continent in eastern Africa, workers dig slabs of salt out of the dried-up lake bed in Ethiopia's Danakil Depression. As they have for centuries, they use primitive tools, often just knives to cut apart the slabs of salt and metal bars or wooden sticks to pry them out. The slabs are cut into smaller chunks to be sold at regional markets. At home people simply cut or scrape some salt off the chunk for cooking or other purposes.

Camel caravans like this one still carry slabs of salt dug up from the salt-encrusted surface of ancient seabeds in Africa's deserts.

In Louisiana's Avery Island mine, one of the largest in the world, bulldozers and other pieces of heavy equipment are dwarfed by the great cavern resulting from mining a salt dome thousands of feet deep.

A modern miner (left background) is dwarfed by this huge burrowing machine, which cuts through underground salt deposits in a mine in Borth, in northern Germany, one of the largest mines in the world.

Underground Salt

Beyond the sea and the land surfaces, vast deposits of salt lie underground. We do not know when people first began to mine salt underground. Long-worked salt mines have been found in Central Europe. One of the most famous was at Hallstatt, a key archaeological site in what is now Austria. Mining there dates back to perhaps 1000 B.C. Salt is a powerful preservative (see p. 17). At Hallstatt it preserved tools, clothing, and even some of the bodies of the miners themselves.

This painting shows part of a saltworks, where salt is extracted by boiling saltwater. It is from the Celtic Museum in Hallein, Austria. The town's name comes from an ancient word for salt, an indication of its long history in making salt.

Some underground mines across Europe and Asia were worked for centuries. Perhaps the most famous is the Wieliczka mine near what is now Cracow, Poland. Worked for more than seven centuries, it has some 190 miles of underground tunnels. Today it is a museum visited by tourists.

Salt mining was brutally difficult. Even today a popular phrase for doing very hard work is "working in the salt mines." Miners had to use muscle power, aided by only a few simple tools, to cut out chunks

of the rock salt. Constant contact with the salt dried out the skin and often caused ulcers (sores) to form.

A different approach to getting salt out of underground deposits was *solution mining*. Water was pumped underground to dissolve some of the salt. The resulting brine was then pumped to the surface and evaporated to extract the salt.

The Chinese pioneered in solution mining, drilling brine wells possibly as early as 250 B.C., centuries before they were used in Europe. Later in Europe some mines

After mining, salt is often handled by large machines, like this mechanical scoop dropping salt into the grid of a storage bin. Originally from a solar salt facility, this salt is being unloaded from a ship and will later be taken to a refinery.

installed giant wheels, turned by workers (often women), to pump the brine out of the mines.

Modern Mining

All of the traditional techniques for extracting salt are still used in some parts of the world, with primitive tools and poorly paid laborers. However, in the main industrial countries mining is now carried out with power-driven machinery and equipment.

In some vast mines, such as Louisiana's Avery Island mines, trucks are dwarfed by the huge caverns from which salt has been removed. Explosives have replaced muscle power in breaking up the rock salt so it can be removed.

A modern technique called *desal-inization* removes salt from seawater to produce drinkable water in regions where water is scarce, as in Saudi Arabia. However, desalinization is still too expensive for wide use, so the amount of salt it produces is small.

Refining Salt

For some purposes, such as melting ice (see p. 28), salt is used as is. It is simply crushed, packaged, and shipped, requiring no processing or refining.

For other purposes, however, salt goes to a refinery. For a time it sometimes simply sits outdoors in huge piles. There it "weathers," as rain falls and cleans the salt somewhat, dissolving away some of the unwanted materials in it. However,

Some countries are enriched with plentiful salt resources in vast deposits underground. People have even carved cathedrals out of the salt in these mines, such as the Zipaquirá Cathedral in Colombia shown here.

too much rain would dissolve the whole pile! That is why many towns place a cover on top of the piles of salt to be used on highways during the winter.

In refineries salt is often dissolved, filtered, dried, and recrystallized. Unwanted matter is removed in the process. Some other things are added, however.

Because salt so readily dissolves in water, it often tends to clump together in rainy or humid weather. Small amounts of other chemicals are added to limit clumping.

Small amounts of iodine are also often added to table salt. The thyroid gland, an organ in the neck that helps regulate many key body functions, requires a small amount of iodine. Without it, the gland overworks and swells, sometimes so much that it causes breathing problems. This enlargement, called a *goiter*, was once common in iodine-poor regions, such as North America's Great Lakes region and Europe's Alps. However, where iodized salt is available, the condition is now rare.

Special Uses of Salt

Most of us think of salt primarily as a seasoning and a food preservative (see p. 17). However, today salt has many other kinds of uses as well. Indeed, perhaps two thirds of current annual salt use is now in industry.

One major use is for deicing. When rock salt (halite) is spread onto ice and snow, it dissolves to form a brine. This salt solution has a lower freezing point than water alone, so it melts the ice and snow. Too much salt can damage roads, vehicles, and plants growing nearby.

Even so, salt is still the most widely used chemical for deicing.

Salt is also very widely used in the chemical industry. Both sodium and chlorine are used in many kinds of chemical compounds. For almost all of them production starts with salt, often as a brine.

Chlorine, for example, is part of many bleaches used to whiten everything from clothes to paper. It is also used in water treatment plants and swimming pools to fight unwanted disease organisms. However, chlorine's main industrial use today is in the production of special chemical compounds. These include carbon tetrachloride and other solvents, which are solutions used to dissolve special materials, and also PVC (polyvinylchloride), a kind of plastic widely used in everything from rain gear to floor tiles to water pipes.

Meanwhile chlorine's partner, sodium, is used in many other kinds of industrial compounds. One such compound is caustic soda (lye), which is used in refining petroleum (oil) and making glass, soaps, paper, and many other products. Another is sodium bicarbonate (baking soda), which is used in baking and also in making carbonated sodas. Sodium hyposulfite is used in photography to "fix" negatives and prints.

For these and many other uses, salt is a basic raw material in industry. Previously worked salt mines themselves have a special use: Being so dry and solid, they are sometimes used for underground storage.

The salt shaker on this table holds the familiar table salt. But salt was also used in manufacturing the glass in the shakers and the wineglass, in making the bleach that whitened the tablecloth and napkin, and possibly in making the glaze on the dishes.

Words to Know

bay salt: See SOLAR SALT.

brine Salty water, as found in the ocean or SALT SPRINGS, or used in preserving and flavoring foods.

cardiovascular system The body's blood-delivery network. If the blood contains too much salt, the body will hold more water, causing the blood to move more forcefully. This causes a condition called *hypertension* or *high blood pressure.*

chlorine: See SODIUM CHLORIDE.

Cl: See NaCL.

crystal A solid form with flat, regularly repeating sides, as in common table salt (see SODIUM CHLORIDE). Salt crystals are generally cubes (boxlike shapes with equal square sides). However, they sometimes form treelike branching crystals called *hopper crystals.* This produces softer *flake salt.*

curing In food preparation to treat foods with salt to dry them out, preserve them, and flavor them.

dehydration Loss of too much water from the body, as through sweat or diarrhea. People must replace not only the water but also other vital substances lost this way, such as SODIUM CHLORIDE.

desalinization Removing salt from seawater to produce drinking water. The operation is too expensive to be a major producer of salt.

evaporation ponds Small pools of saltwater exposed to the sun, so water will *evaporate* (go into the air), leaving salt CRYSTALS behind.

flake salt: See CRYSTAL.

halite The chemical name for salt in rock form, as in underground deposits or surface deposits, such as SALT FLATS.

high blood pressure: See CARDIOVASCULAR SYSTEM.

hopper crystal: See CRYSTAL.

hormones Chemicals that the body produces to perform certain functions. Some hormones help control the amount of salt in the body.

hypertension: See CARDIOVASCULAR SYSTEM.

NaCl The chemical abbreviation for SODIUM CHLORIDE. *Na* is an abbreviation for natron, a French word for salt, and *Cl* is the abbreviation for *chlorine.*

peat Matted masses of partly decayed vegetable matter. Peat formed in saltwater bogs can be burned and the ashes mixed with water to extract the salt.

precipitation In chemistry, formation of a solid within a liquid solution, as when salt CRYSTALS form in very salty water.

refining Removing impurities. At saltworks this usually involves dissolving the salt, filtering it, and then evaporating the water to get CRYSTALS of salt.

saline Salty. Saline solutions are sometimes given to medical patients in cases of DEHYDRATION.

saltcellar A small dish for holding salt, in a kitchen or on a dining table.

salt dome A large underground deposit of salt that has been pushed up between other rocks near the surface, where it can be mined. Oil (petroleum) is often found nearby.

salt flats The dried-up remains of ancient seabeds, the saltwater often leaving behind large deposits of salt.

salt lick A natural deposit of salt or a block provided by humans that animals lick to get SODIUM CHLORIDE.

salt springs Inland water sources that contain large amounts of salt from dissolving salt in nearby rocks; also called *brine springs.* SALTWORKS are often established nearby.

saltworks A place where salt is produced, such as where BRINE is boiled for salt or raked out of EVAPORATION PONDS.

sea salt: See SOLAR SALT.

sodium chloride The chemical name for common table salt. It is a compound (mixed substance) made of the elements (basic substances) sodium and chlorine (see NACL). Sodium chloride is generally found in CRYSTAL form but readily dissolves in water.

solar salt Salt formed as water vaporizes out of EVAPORATION PONDS. When produced on seacoasts, also called *sea salt* or *bay salt.*

solution mining The process of pumping water into underground deposits to dissolve salt and then pumping out the resulting BRINE and extracting the salt.

On the Internet

The Internet has many interesting sites about salt. The site addresses often change, so the best way to find current addresses is to go to a search site, such as www.yahoo.com. Type in a word or phrase, such as "salt" or "sodium chloride."

As this book was being written, websites about salt included:

http://www.saltinstitute.org/
The Salt Institute, offering wide-ranging information on salt and its sources, history, production, and uses, plus a teaching unit on "Salt: The Essence of Life."

http://www.saltinfo.com/
The Salt Manufacturers' Association, website from the British organization, offering information, history, and more.

http://www.lionsaltworkstrust.co.uk/
The Lion Saltworks Trust, website of a British saltworks converted into a museum, offering history and details of producing salt by evaporation.

http://www.salt.org.il/links.html
Common Salt (NaCl), a collection of links to salt-related websites, including salt museums around the world and a wide range of articles.

In Print

Your local library system will have various books on salt. The following is just a sampling of them.

Adshead, Samuel Adrian M. *Salt and Civilization*. New York: St. Martin's, 1992.

Denton, Derek A. *The Hunger for Salt: An Anthropological, Physiological, and Medical Analysis*. Berlin; New York: Springer-Verlag, 1982.

Froman, Robert. *The Science of Salt*. New York: McKay, 1967.

Kraske, Robert. *Crystals of Life: The Story of Salt*. Garden City, NY: Doubleday, 1968.

Kurlansky, Mark. *Salt: A World History*. London: Jonathan Cape, 2002.

Laszlo, Pierre. *Salt: Grain of Life*. New York: Columbia University Press, 2001.

MacGregor, Graham A., and Hugh E. de Wardener. *Salt, Diet and Health*. Cambridge, UK: Cambridge University Press, 1998.

Multhauf, Robert P. *Neptune's Gift: A History of Common Salt*. Baltimore, MD: Johns Hopkins University Press, 1978.

Salt: The Mysterious Necessity. Mark Batterson and William W. Boddie, eds. Midland, MI: Dow Chemical Co., 1972.

Schulkin, Jay. *Sodium Hunger: The Search for a Salty Taste*. New York: Cambridge University Press, 1991.

Shepard, Sue. *Pickled, Potted, and Canned*. New York: Simon & Schuster, 2000.

Tisdale, Sallie. *Lot's Wife: Salt and the Human Condition*. New York: Holt, 1988.

Van Nostrand's Scientific Encyclopedia, 8th ed., 2 vols. Douglas M. Considine and Glenn D. Considine, eds. New York: Van Nostrand Reinhold, 1995.

Index